Heliopause

Wesleyan University Press ►

▼ Middletown, Connecticut

Wesleyan University Press

Middletown CT 06459

www.wesleyan.edu/wespress

© 2015 Heather Christle

All rights reserved

Manufactured in the United States of America

Designed and typeset in Whitman

by Eric M. Brooks

ART WORKS.

*This project is supported in part by an award from
the National Endowment for the Arts*

Wesleyan University Press is a member of the
Green Press Initiative. The paper used in this
book meets their minimum requirement for
recycled paper.

Library of Congress
Cataloging-in-Publication Data
Christle, Heather, 1980–
[Poems. Selections]
Heliopause / Heather Christle.
     pages; cm.—(Wesleyan poetry series)
ISBN 978-0-8195-7529-6 (hardcover)—
ISBN 978-0-8195-7530-2 (ebook)
I. Title.
PS3603.H755A6   2015
811'.6—dc23   2014044266

5 4 3 2 1

■ for Harriet

What is the language using us for?
It uses us all and in its dark
Of dark actions selections differ.

I am not making a fool of myself
For you. What I am making is
A place for language in my life

Which I want to be a real place
Seeing I have to put up with it
Anyhow.

▲ W. S. Graham

Contents

▲

▲

▲

▲

▲

Heliopause

A Perfect Catastrophe

To have stood midfield among the vast and livid green
and never heard the grasses take their vow of silence
is experience, not evidence, and meanwhile clouds descend

and buffer light. When did I arrive? I recall it came on
slowly as a fever as a poem is a communicable *please.*
What's in charge here is the scattered light all over

and how it pulls my very blood into my hands
until they graph a fat *what* the sun likes holding
and some dumb mutter good and nails me to the bone.

Disintegration Loop 1.1

····································

■ *for William Basinski*

In seeking to resolve a conflict
between two parties
                    one can assume
each believes it is acting
in good faith
                just as the hopeful
gravel waits for your rough step

▲

The only way to be truly alone
is for there to be nothing

not even myself

▲

In looping you rephrase after listening
to what the person has to say

what the person had to say

and having the new words affirmed
you wait and listen again

▲

Myself the eager magnet
for another to address

▲

Maybe I should think this a spiral
a loop that gets closer
a loop that will not close

▲

To make nothing
draw a circle
around what isn't there

▲

I found a note I left in the corner
of a part of the poem we rarely used

If you ever feel trapped
                              it said
this is where to escape

▲

But legally I owe you nothing
I owe you at least that much

▲

Like being haunted by the spirit of the letter

▲

I remember my teacher's story
of two teenagers who died in a blizzard
trying to stay warm
                              and the tailpipe
blocked with snow

so I always check

but it still happens
                    just yesterday
a man's young son in what the paper
called *one awful story*

▲

The light switch has a beautiful feeling
when a person reaches out to make it change

and the warm quadrangles of sun
on the carpet are beautiful too
and red berries on the gray bush
and the mail as long as it lasts

and beauty is what beauty does to you

▲

Like trying to say a seagull
inscribing a circle

over what land
the day has thought
to provide

▲

to enter into agreement with yourself
to lie but only out of love
for the verblessness of buildings

They do not rise except once
and then nothing
                    how being is nothing
and if there were a word after
it would be a slow decay

▲

I will love across any distance
you think this has made to occur

▲

Nothing so ruthless as a life

▲

The day hangs low overhead
and soon enough the new grass will emerge
through the gravel

They have big plans to meet
in the middle
                    and in so doing
to phase all this out

▲

I go on
            say enough and it will blur
off into sound
                    look up and see that night
has nearly settled in and darkness

and hope that if I look into it
long enough and keep my mouth
quiet
            when I look down again I'll find
a settled word
                    to which nothing
is attached

▲

Re: the day
          someone said
what doesn't kill you makes it longer

▲

It's like footsteps toward you
that sound for all the world like
they forever move away

▲

I keep forgetting I'm the smoke
not the camera
                    Then I see my dark
joining sky to what's below

▲

Like watching someone
from across a river
                    on such a clear day
that you can see her teeth
                    and at such
a distance
          that you can't hear the sound

so while you know
it must be screaming
                    it is possible
to imagine her faraway mouth

which you can see but not save

has opened—is open—to sing

▲

After the collapse and before
the dust settles
                the darkness billows
and grows
            like it's describing
itself to the sky
                this it says
this and much bigger
                        but the sky
in its sorrow
                has had to turn away

▲

to expect praise for the beautiful apology

▲

to imagine something other than again

▲

Whether it is falling
from a ship
                or plane or a building
the human body starts its drop
at roughly one rate

▲

The book said legally
                    thought the captain
of the slave ship *Zong*
                    to throw the people overboard
instead of letting them starve
would ensure compensation
                        for his loss

▲

And another has made
the words to decay

until what remains
is
　　loss　*loss*

▲

When I go to the video
it is paused close to darkness
the place
　　　　where I had last stopped
and as I drag the cursor backward
so it can start again
　　　　　　I'm reversing
into morning what was night

▲

The three buildings in the corner
begin a hypotenuse
　　　　　　the dark clouds
—diligent—complete

▲

The subsection of sympathy cards
labeled *words fail me*
　　　　　on which we pen
sorry for your loss

▲

The lights that come on last—
what were they resisting?

Or do they not notice
as sometimes can happen

while the hours carry in
the new-fallen dark

▲

They say we have *fallen*
a long way
                to the cold
and planetary light

▲

They say *the bomb is a flower*

▲

A body falls much faster
than the night

▲

You will forgive me won't you
for the lines
                I'm copying in
I do not want to be alone here
despite what I have said

▲

And I have forgotten
to mention the music

though it has this whole time
been mentioning me

I will say it is the sound of a clock
which has had all of its hours removed

▲

The screen is dark enough now
that it can perfectly reflect
the facing window
                    a corner of morning

▲

And some of the lights
                    they tremble
trying to decide
                    whether they can go on

▲

Lights like pronouns for the buildings

▲

to remove to go through to withdraw
to slowly walk into another room

▲

What is legally an hour?
The time it takes the king
to fall asleep
                    the melting
of a candle in the snow

▲

Hour like *a jar in Tennessee*

▲

And yes *I am afraid*
to be with minutes

They have completely confused me

▲

The buildings are a sort
of interference
                              how they stand
and complicate the sky

but nothing interferes
with the hour
                    it is
as they say
                 a law
unto itself

▲

Maybe I should say that
                              I am sitting
in a room
                 different from
the one you are in now

and I am sitting at a distance
from the screen
                         so that the hour
goes on
              and there is nothing
that I can undo

▲

Every morning the diminishing returns

▲

And now the smoke echoes the roundness
of the one building with a dome

the smoke in love and unable
to do anything more than repeat

the words of another

so after *I would sooner be dead*
than let you touch me
                              it cries hopeless
touch me
touch me

and then even that sound
                              that shape
drifts away

▲

If I could get closer I could see
the river
          reflecting back
the buildings' light
                    but I am placed *here*
at this fixed distance
and the lights are fixed *there*

in the permanently imminent night

▲

I know there are other cities
                        other hours
where you can watch the lights
copying themselves
                all neoned and strobe-hearted

▲

I know *all our yesterdays have lighted fools*
the way to dusky death

▲

Today the reflected window
seems stupid
                and too bright

replacing smoke with the pale sky
and the tree
                its bare branches
a cracking explosion

no eye could resist

▲

to justify desires with omens

▲

to walk away before the morning ends

▲

I'm counting my life
I'm counting the buildings

one   one   two

▲

If you are in the center it means
every edge you can imagine
is the very same distance away

▲

If this is my home
                    If this is my screen
If these are my books
                    imagined companions

▲

This is the city
I can describe it
                    black
with power

an electricity
                    forced into light

Vernon Street

At that time they made
the telephone in order
to say
  Come here
I need you
   and nothing
has changed except
here now you are
and I
  in order in
the order
that's arranged this child
who passes now
    and answers
an unheard question
     It means
when your life is bad
and you are dying
you are running down a hill
going
  and then the boy screams

Next time I will live
my life in alphabetical order
Come here I need you
There are ways
   to settle down
There's an accidental light
the grass is showing

and my cat
            is so sad
that the house right now
divides us
            He is in
the window crying
but I am needed outside
where I have
ordered myself
            where I half
expect your voice
to turn me over
                  and up
there the quiet sky the plane
is bringing noise to
above my head and in it
I need to show
you this
            Come here come here

Summer

Today you find yourself guilty
as the rim you split
an egg against
You press charges
You spell out your name
like the letters are medals
for good conduct in a bad war
The night moves in with you
into your room
until even your sleep
is not your own
Through the window
the grass tells you
to give up
and you are trying
but on the other hand
things keep you:
the moon, the cars, cars
You undress yourself
more deeply down
like this is the way
to get to the future
You let the darkness
medically examine you
So much can't be
put back together
To burn the house down
to burn the house up

It's the same problem
in any direction
You're matter
You turn on the light

Realistic Flowers

At the dollar store I bought
a bouquet of fake flowers
and what could have been
but somehow (incredibly) wasn't
It only cost $2 but still
that did not help
                    I planted
the flowers among actual flowers
b/c what else can you do
I was so happy I could have
torn your head apart

I Am Glad of Your Arrival

Addressing the morning I say
it was good of you to come

                                 as if
it were the sole visitor amidst scandal
when in fact

                    it has been endless
with the trees and grass and cars
and the cowbell someone's using
as a wind chime

                    in the winds
just remnants of the storm
that wouldn't stay

                      I have thought
to run away from what I own
Who hasn't

                  but what else do I have
Where would I go

                    The sky is everywhere
at once like a big movie
and though I think I know how
it's going to end

                    and with which music
there is uncertainty enough
to hold me still

It's an Empire Out There

I saw you walk
past the window box
and brush against
one flower
        I saw you
readjust your jacket
saw you kiss
           Long live
whatever needs our dying
Whatever feeds us
             and then
tells us *don't exist*

Elegy for Neil Armstrong

Neil

all systems   over

No, hold it just a minute

Okay,

Okay,
a little more

for your TV

Neil,   You're

                                    a picture
on the TV
        Oh

                                Neil, we can
see you

                                get   up

mankind   is fine
and powdery, I can pick it up
loosely with my toe

            I can

here –   here   I
    see
         the descent

Over.

Neil?

I'm with you.

…   (garbled)

…

    I'm standing directly in the
shadow now

everything
is sufficiently bright,

everything is very clearly
    Okay

It's … I'm

a long way out
Buzz?

I …
I have no flags
I'm in minimum flow

                                          clear and spiderly

Are you getting a
picture now, Houston?
Yes, Neil, we are getting a
picture

Neil,

                                    You've got
              three more steps and then a long
              one   A little more
                                                         There, you got it.
                                              That's a good step

                    There you go

And This Too Comes Apart

People agree with sleep
They nod into it
but death they sometimes fight off
until they can't
                    and then
from their graves
they stick out their tongues

Good for them
Good for the people

In the world I can see
there is one tree still raining
The sun blares around
                        lights it up
in lines alongside the spiders'

They have an arrangement
a private design

When I'm arranged
into a mother
I will name my child
Incredulity and like it so much
I'll do it again
                three or four
or eight times

Stand up!
Good and straight like a tree
good and stiff like
the rain-darkened gravestone
perpendicular
                    to the quiet

Or sit down
and make a nice lap
nod Incredulity off into sleep

Enumerate to her the lines
of the song you haven't meant yet

Hatch

In every place
you seem to end
I have loved you

There was that small
and dead and pink
bird we saw

near the sidewalk
with its smashed
open mouth

a place to let
the world in
a way of not ending

I loved you so
I had to crawl inside

Such and Such a Time at Such and Such a Palace

The lack of a single-word infinitive
in our language is what is killing me

this morning
                    A single word for all
infinitives is what God is doing tonight

This is just one of many acts
to have passed through the garden

Previously on this show they put
a peacock back together wrong

after its demise
                    Something
there was in the syntax

Poor bird could feel it in his bones

Me and My Head as Pieces of Wood

Please accept my uselessness
as a token of other letters

a   b   a   c   u   s

spells an occasional
way to be feeling

There are limits
                    These are
my limitations

I spin around I can't
slide back to then

Flowers Are Also Letters

Imagine eating
in one bite
a rose
     or
imagine eating
gold
    manger de l'or
Do I?
    Do I ever!
O *e* !
   O *i* !
O *e i e i o* !

Nature Poem

Yesterday it was marsh marigolds
by the river with my mother
and in the afternoon forsythia
with Chris
        (he dislikes it)
and today it is grass again
with ants departing
           or heading
toward each other to exchange
an urgent message
        Church bells
are literally ringing and then
oh my god the train
         and jesus christ a butterfly
lovely brown with off-white tips
and every now and then irregular
lavender spots
       It's not necessary
to write everything down

When a creature quietly tends
to itself
      I am happy
and by extension earlier I thought
for actually a very long time

about ants and the impossibility
of ant masturbation

They do not love themselves enough
They only love each other

They Are Leaving You a Message

■ *for Arda Collins*

What they are trying to tell you
is you are wearing the wrong bra
for your shape and situation
This might not even be your life
and in the midst of my thinking
to tell you this a fruit fly
has begun to trail me through the house
as if I were its mother or as if
it were the other way around
and it always is and the house
is on fire at some point
in the simultaneity and I am leaving it
to buy all the things I do
and do not devour

Drapes

They were erecting a conversation
in the middle of the inconsequential
afternoon
        like one of those unnatural flowers
you drop into water and watch
immediately blossom
           And then then what
Has anything changed?
They were emigrating from one wall
to the other
        like swans of
ungodly proportions
           They were not so much
humans as blood drenched with hair

Uncloudy

Sitting in the tower munching clover
with no roof
          with encircled sky
a dark hole the quick stars infest

I need these stones to quiet me down
I need the quiet so nouns can collect

The clover's a pulp
              as if I'm making paper
lifting up linen strips from who else
but the dead
          And never has this star clutch
been so silent
          Forever have I darkly thee undressed

Not Much More Room in the Cemetery

I will lie down on top of the graves
It will never feel okay and that is the point
People beneath and people behind me
with their faces and their little horns
and the places from which they are shining
I know there is something else
that they have tried to teach me
and I am sorry for all of the times
I have listened and not learned it
No I am not crying
I'm maybe   um   a demon
For certain I am waving this fruit fly away

As If No Light Could Warm You

A person in
a nice dress

She moves
into the shape

the sun makes
on the floor

A nice dress
& it clamors

A voice says
I can take it

She says *I*
take it back

How Long Is the Heliopause

They say before you know you want
to move your hand
                    your hand
is already about to move
They say in advance
                    these things
are decided

The box of cereal says *We're so happy*
our paths have crossed
                    but I do not think
I am on one
            I think I am in
a pathless field

The wind sends seeds abroad
                            The most careful engineering
Still these contrary gardens grow

They say it is hard to believe
that when robots are taking pictures

of Titan's orange ethane lakes
poets still insist on writing about their divorces

This is a poem for my husband
on the occasion of *Voyager*

        perhaps having left our solar system
perhaps about to leave it very soon

          They cannot say
The message takes so long to drift to reach us

When the self-driving car wants to move
it will first say so

    changing lanes

        changing lanes

            changing lanes

It hesitates it does not know it is lost
or it has decided on always changing

I've heard the cat who may be alive
or may be dead should expect
to live forever

      progressively growing
sicker and sicker

This is for my husband
whom I expect to come home
some time between now and the future

Let me date this very clearly
This is the year after the year
when people with cable began
to pile Christmas lights into glass jars

the year of evidence of chemical warfare
clear or uncertain
                    depending on where you live

One beast lives one grows sicker and sicker
One dies one yowls at the door

Two days from now I will either
bleed or not bleed
                    I will remember
that four years ago we wed and asked
for Divine Assistance
                        though we neither of us
pray to any god

This is for him on the occasion
of the Olympian's indictment

They say he shot
the one he loved
                    Shot the one
who through a door
                        he could not see

None of this has been right
but maybe a tiny electrical god
has cut and spliced us together

And in this moment yes and in this moment no
and in this moment all the lights
go off at once and it is a bomb
or it is a daughter

And this great sound replaces the others
so I can hear nothing but the brightness
of the field
                    where I am waiting for the warm chest
of my husband
                    for its occasion
and if they say a word now
it would take years for me to know

Some Glamorous Country

In the war's geometry
among the many givens
the spaces of the torn
away limbs articulate
what
          What are they
needed to prove

On the sidewalk
I'm watching a full-length
animation the trees made
w/technical direction
from the sun

We saw *Batman* at
a matinee because who
would bother to shoot
so few so early in the day

It is not that my life
has become interesting
to me
          It is that
given the terrified world
how can I
                    & can I resist

the things I have done
in my name

In the Dumps

Just because we've broken my head
doesn't mean we must glue it together
There's other work to be done
                              and dark
grass freezing
                There is some old light
to read by and large pink thumbs
And with my head apart
                        I think
the world can get in easy
                        This
pound of dirt I'm holding weighs a ton

Pursuits

It is not that you want
to be the one to make prints
in the untrampled snow
It is that you want
to be in the snow
without having touched it
to be of the snow
not beginning
Everywhere commerce
dictates the shapes
that move you along
that seat you at a table
far from the snow
far from the act
of not touching
It only gets worse
A girl's gotta eat
And your hunger's
not even your own

Aesthetics of Crying

You meet someone and later you meet
their dancing
                        and you have to start again
You like cat one
                        and you like cat two
and they do terrible things to each other

Once to celebrate a bad mood
we broke all the clean dishes

There are pictures
                        I'd like a portrait
of an angry horse with his beauty
and his fuming
                        It's hard to know
what you look like when you're mad

Crying's easier
                        I have cried at times
for so long that I have moved the activity
in front of the mirror
                                out of curiosity
The information I gathered there remains
thus far unused
                        but let the record show
my horrible face

Keep in Shape

I only think the snow regards me
It falls where I stand
                    and that's all
It doesn't stay in place when I
walk on
           They say Jesus wrote
a little in some dirt that
blew away
             They say a man
can piss a short name
in the snow
               Nice work
See me after class
                  See how
the weather does not write me
never phones
               I can't pretend
that doesn't hurt
                 but I can
pretend I'm burning down my home

Optioned

Of my days I'm director
not author
                and neither of us has
any money

I was born with a wooden spoon
in my ass
                Imagine my embarrassment!
Then go ahead and imagine your own

What does a house do?
                        That's easy
It houses
                just as a cloud
pulls the light from a face
when someone utters *mortgage*

In any other world
                        a sweet name
for a daughter
                        beginning as it does
with a little death

Annual

The sky lifted from black into paleness
while gloom rocked the markets
gently
        a terrifying dad

I had intended to have flowers
delivered
           It was a condition
I'd suffered before

 On the back road
you remarked upon the width
of the stone wall and everyone nodded
walked slowly away

 Our lives are I think
coming apart
           There were clouds
we could see but not say

Ecumene

We are where we are bound for
where life is still motion and we
have seen a rabbit seen a river
seen the rope
                  Two times we slept
in Virginia when mountains gathered
themselves for the light
It was pink and then darker
into a lilac no trouble to like

All of the time now we have to imagine
the children of our friends
                          Impossible people
how they go on and how other
times they end by these trees and
oh by their shadows
                     the dark uncovered places
of now becoming a then

Dear Seth

■ *for Seth Landman*

Dear Seth

        You have been disappointed
in love and I am sorry
                that to hope
for and to imagine love is to possess it
however briefly
             so that when the picture
does not come clear one experiences
not only sadness but loss
                We had an appointment
These dumb risks of ours these dumb arms
How aversion is the urge to look away
I know the general uselessness
of looking to words for answers
                    but on occasion
the cast spell works
            so we still mutter
what we can
        We stutter *Try*

Dear Seth

        It's snowing again lightly in Ohio
like it had an idea and thought
There's no harm
            in trying it out
before growing distracted
by some town I cannot see
For you in Massachusetts I hope
for enough weather
                that the office gives up
and tells you to stay home
Do you remember the day we drove
out to the gorge?
          I could not see
the difference between the pale sky
and the ground
          like the snow
had erased the whole horizon
It was a good day and I miss you
I hope you are well

Dear Seth

          There is fear the baby
when it arrives will be wrongly
or poorly loved
                    that the world is no place
for helpless things
                    You will see
reading this through your good beard
how neatly
          I have left myself out
though I understand
                    come spring
such grammar tricks
will no longer work

Dear Seth

       Yesterday was Thanksgiving
and for you Hanukkah
          At dinner
with acquaintances my joke
about terminal illness did not go over well

and the small spark I'd hoped to kindle
in myself went dark
         Of the many
things I miss about your company
today most keenly I think
of us laughing at death
            knowing
and not minding that death laughs back

Dear Seth

        I love your long-standing appreciation
for the *Voyager* mission
                  whose equipment
is now very old
            When I imagine the adolescent you
delivering the science fair spiel
I picture the body as you now
                    reproduced
at a four-fifths scale
the way they used to paint the child Christ

before looking more carefully
at the actual young
            Neil Armstrong died
the same day *Voyager* finally reached the limit
of our solar system
              as you know
Thanks to him we better see
how to go about painting the moon

Dear Seth

        I am still thinking about space
For a long time they did not know
if *Voyager* had crossed the heliopause
and we lived
        in the strange interim
of an event perhaps having occurred
in the uncertainty of something
having happened
        without knowing what
It is like wondering which body part
has begun to kill us
        Chris is very worried
about his eyes
        his mismatched pupils
but I think and say they're probably just fine

Dear Seth

       Now Chris is visiting you
in Northampton and the house around
me exists
       just one room at a time
Nelson Mandela has died
The radio
       can think of little else
You would not believe my pride
at having shoveled the driveway
My shame
       when I fail
to start the fire
       I am actually
alive inside this mythic air
a child assigns
       to the time
before its birth
Were there a proverb for this week
it'd go a little like
       He who lives
inside a snowglobe always drowns

Dear Seth

                    Watching *Frances Ha* the other night
I fell into the panic of my old New York life
with all its drinking
                              and so little money
Representations of debt terrify me more
than those of sickness
                              I would love to draft a chart
of my heart rate when reading *Madame Bovary*

Last night success in building the fire
and Chris has come home happy
                              as I knew
you would make him
                              The first night he ate
fried chicken and you ordered pork chops
and these are real plates of food
that make me feel strong and alive
                              If only
I could think as tenderly of myself
as I do of you and of my former selves!
but this is not the case
                              and therefore not a part
of the everything that we still call the world
like the soot on my hands
                              the voice on the air
or the desk where you sit again today

Dear Seth

        I was going to say the alphabet
is perfect but I think I mean sufficient
which is better
              is enough
In my sleep I did something to my back
and here at 5 am I am up
                    trying to think
of a word
          that brings nothing else to mind

Dear Seth

       We are in the new year now
hello
    In the last days of the old one
the doctor told us hard news
              and my mind excluded
most other thoughts
         so when the idea
to make that joke about your book came to me
I was grateful for the visit

And it's true that almost nothing is better
than the movies
        Philomena   *American Hustle*
or a series is good
        Tinker Tailor Soldier Spy
On New Year's Eve a new test told us
we'd all probably be okay

 I did not know
when I began I'd fill these poems
with so much information
           which saturates
my life
    Some people see information
as that which cannot be predicted
           the break

in the pattern
               It is still snowing
I'd like to know how this year
will break me

Dear Seth

        I have been thinking
about the department stores
of our previous century

                how they enchanted us
with stacks of televisions broadcasting
novel images of ourselves

              walking through the store
I would wave and jump
I'd never heard of nonchalance
but now there is no place

            that does not see you
and we have learned to act naturally
all the time

      It's not that we forget
the camera's there

         It's that we struggle
to recall anything else

Dear Seth

          Chris has a terrible cold
and is still sleeping
                  while I awoke
stupidly early once again
                     I am dissatisfied
with everything I read
and therefore with myself
Today I think I'll take down
                      the pine wreathes
and garlands
            I will finish up shoveling the drive
Tomorrow the baby hits the size
of a banana
          which reminds me
to buy some for Chris
                 (He is crazy for bananas)
I want them to make him feel well

Dear Seth

        Last night we tried to go see *Her*
but after dinner the snow sent us home
                           and here
before dawn I am up thinking of how much
you love the Celtics and *Moby Dick*
                        One August we ate
birthday cake in Herman Melville's barn
                           Your stomach
is as weak as your heart is steadfast

Henri Bergson says the comic stems
from a certain absent-mindedness

At your house
            when we would watch a game
I'd amuse myself pretending to forget
there was a ball
            but your understanding
travels broader
and more deeply
            You read the bright screen
as a whale would read the swells

Where I see a general blur you see particular shapes
and this is why the game to you must be called tragic

It is too early to go find regular paper
so I am writing this

                         on the back of a letter
from BlueCross BlueShield
No action is required on your part

Poem for Bill Cassidy

Already I have confessed
the whole alphabet
                          under my own duress
I came back again to try
a lamentation
                          perhaps to put out
a match on my wet tongue
It goes out and I
do not go with it
                          There are marks
I find hard to erase

▲

But think how grand it would be
to glide as casual as the sun!
                          shining
light in mild trapezoids along
the floor or hill
                          For that kind of work I'd need
the most expensive dresses
Among this and that I also lack money
So I will occupy myself
with keeping bees
                          or whatever
Is there a name that makes honey
I will write it
                          I don't care
I've done worse

▲

Last night apparently a sunset
I missed
            Instead I received some light instruction
Imagine pink imagine pink imagine orange
I can pronounce it
                        but I do not understand
How do you say over
How do you say again
                            They put the sun back
in the ocean where it's kept

▲

I will consider this milk
                            I mean confess it
Tell me the funniest thing
                        I'll spit it out

▲

A green thought or a mind of winter
Had I either one I'd gladly put it out
I swear I'd plate it!
                    But I have only
this green tongue this wet mouth
There's no detaching them
                        and look it's back
the sun

▲

You know how indigo
                    the word
threatens always to tear off

into its pieces
                  When you die
that's the first thing to go
I am guessing
                 You'd have to ask Bill
Hey Bill
        where you are
do you see letters

How long do we wait before we say
there's no reply
                given how slowly
these black words will drift to reach him
given all this thick light
                   given how time

Notes and Acknowledgments

The epigraph to this book is taken from the second poem in
W. S. Graham's sequence, "What Is the Language Using Us For?"

"Disintegration Loop 1.1"

I wrote this poem over several weeks, waking each morning and playing
William Basinski's video of lower Manhattan, recorded during the last
hour of daylight on September 11, 2001. The accompanying music is a
"decaying pastoral loop Basinski . . . recorded in August 2001." While
the music and video played across the room, I sat in a chair with my
paper and wrote for the full hour. Or rather, I sat for an hour and wrote
when it occurred to me to do so. The poem is full of lines and ideas from
friends and books, for whom and which I am very grateful.

Thank you, Jess Fjeld, for telling me about looping and conflict
resolution.

Thank you, Robert Kaplan, for introducing me to the history of zero.

Thank you, M. NourbeSe Philip, for creating *Zong!*, and thank you,
Cathy Park Hong, for alerting me to its existence.

Thank you, Jen Bervin, for catching "loss / loss" in your *Nets*.

Thank you, Sylvia Plath, for the "light of the mind, cold and planetary."

Thank you, William Carlos Williams, for seeing "the bomb is a flower."

Thank you, Wallace Stevens, for placing that jar.

Thank you, Matvei Yankelevich, for bringing Alexander Vvedensky's
minutes and confusion into English.

Thank you, Alvin Lucier, for sitting in a room.

Thank you, Ted Hughes, for remaking Ovid's tale of Echo and Narcissus.

Thank you, Anne Sexton, for watching "the lights copying themselves, / all neoned and strobe-hearted."

Thank you, William Shakespeare, for "all our yesterdays."

Thank you, Dana Inez, for reminding me of the geometric definition of "center."

More than anything, thank you, William Basinski, for your music.

"Vernon Street"

According to the March 10, 1896, notebook entry of Alexander Graham Bell, the first words to be spoken and understood over the telephone were in fact "Mr. Watson—come here—I want to see you."

"Elegy for Neil Armstrong"

This poem was created by erasing a transcript of communications between mission control, Neil Armstrong, and Buzz Aldrin during the first moon landing. I found the transcript in *Things Working*, a book in the Penguin English Project published in 1970 and edited by Penny Blackie. As here, in the original pages the text appeared in white against a black background.

"How Long Is the Heliopause"

"We're so happy our paths have crossed" quotes a box of Nature's Path Organic Heritage Flakes I bought and then ate.

"They say it is hard to believe / that when robots are taking pictures // of Titan's orange ethane lakes / poets still insist on writing about their divorces" refers to one of Christian Bök's tweets from September 8, 2012. Many of his tweets begin with the word "they."

The lines about "The cat who may be alive / or may be dead" are based on my misunderstanding of the philosopher David Lewis's paper, "How Many Lives Has Schrodinger's Cat?" as explained to me by the poet-philosopher Larisa Svirsky.

"Some Glamorous Country"

The title of this poem borrows from Frank O'Hara's "Ave Maria."

"Keep in Shape"

This poem refers to a passage in the New Testament (John 8:1–8), in which Jesus writes on the ground of a temple. It is the only story of him writing instead of speaking aloud. The King James translation renders it thus:

> Jesus went unto the mount of Olives.
>
> And early in the morning he came again into the temple, and all the people came unto him; and he sat down, and taught them.
>
> And the scribes and Pharisees brought unto him a woman taken in adultery; and when they had set her in the midst,
>
> They say unto him, Master, this woman was taken in adultery, in the very act.
>
> Now Moses in the law commanded us, that such should be stoned: but what sayest thou?
>
> This they said, tempting him, that they might have to accuse him. But Jesus stooped down, and with *his* finger wrote on the ground, *as though he heard them not.*
>
> So when they continued asking him, he lifted up himself, and said unto them, He that is without sin among you, let him first cast a stone at her.
>
> And again he stooped down, and wrote on the ground.

"Poem for Bill Cassidy"

Bill Cassidy was a poet and my friend. He died in 2011.

"A green thought" belongs to Andrew Marvell.

The "mind of winter" and the "green tongue" belong to Wallace Stevens.

▲

Thank you to everyone mentioned above, as well as to Michele Christle, Christopher DeWeese, Lisa Olstein, Emily Pettit, and Suzanna Tamminen, for whose careful reading I am grateful.

Thanks also to the editors of the following journals, where some of these poems first appeared: *Barrelhouse, Better, Burnside Review, Colorado Review, Everyday Genius, Fanzine, LIT, Mead, Octopus,* and *Poetry*.

Thank you to Emily Bludworth de Barrios, Emily Pettit, Guy Pettit, and Dara Wier at Factory Hollow Press, for publishing some of these poems in the chapbook *Private Party*.

Thank you to Christopher Louvet at Floating Wolf Quarterly for publishing *Dear Seth* as an e-chapbook.

■ Heather Christle is the author of three previous poetry collections. She has taught writing at Antioch College, Sarah Lawrence College, Emory University, and the University of Massachusetts Amherst, where she received her MFA. A native of Wolfeboro, New Hampshire, she now lives in Yellow Springs, Ohio, where she is writing a book about crying.